TO SHINE ONE CORNER OF THE WORLD

TO
SHINE ONE
CORNER
OF
THE WORLD

moments with Shunryu Suzuki

stories of a zen master told by his students

edited by David Chadwick

Broadway Books · *New York*

TO SHINE ONE CORNER OF THE WORLD. Copyright © 2001 by David Chadwick. All rights reserved. Printed in the United States of America. No part of this book may be reproduced or transmitted in any form or by any means, electronic or mechanical, including photocopying, recording, or by any information storage and retrieval system, without written permission from the publisher. For information, address Broadway Books, a division of Random House, Inc., 1540 Broadway, New York, NY 10036.

Broadway Books titles may be purchased for business and promotional use or for special sales. For information, please write to: Special Markets Department, Random House, Inc., 1540 Broadway, New York, NY 10036.

BROADWAY BOOKS and its logo, a letter B bisected on the diagonal, are trademarks of Broadway Books, a division of Random House, Inc.

Visite our Web site at www.broadwaybooks.com

Library of Congress Cataloging-in-Publication Data:
To shine one corner of the world: moments with Shuryu Suzuki / the students of Shunryu Suzuki; edited by David Chadwick,--1st ed.
p. cm.
Includes bibliographical references.
ISBN 0-7679-0651-9
1. Suzuki, Shunryu, 1904---Quotations. 2. Spiritual life--Zen Buddhism--Quotations, maxims, etc. 1. Chadwick, David, 1945-

BQ988.U9 T6 2001
294.3'927'092--dc21   00-045506
FIRST EDITION

Designed by Jenny Wunderly

01 02 03 04 10 9 8 7 6 5 4 3 2 1

Contents

They may forget what you said,

but they will never forget how you made them feel.

CARL W. BUECHNER

Introduction

Shunryu Suzuki Roshi, a Soto Zen priest from Japan, arrived in San Francisco in 1959 at the age of fifty-five. He came to minister to a congregation of Japanese Americans at a temple on Bush Street in Japantown called Sokoji, Soto Zen Mission. *His* mission, however, was more than what his hosts had in mind for him. He brought his dream of introducing to the West the practice of the wisdom and enlightenment of the Buddha, as he had learned it from his teachers. To those who were attracted to the philosophy of Zen, he brought something to do—*zazen* (Zen meditation), and *Zen practice* (the extension of zazen into daily life). A community of students soon formed around him; many of them moved into apartments in the neighborhood so that they could walk to Sokoji for zazen in the early mornings and evenings.

In 1964 a small group of students began to meet for daily zazen in Los Altos, south of San Francisco. Other groups formed in Mill Valley and Berkeley. Suzuki Roshi, as he was called, would join each one once a week, when he could. He lived exclusively at Sokoji until 1967, when Zen Mountain Center was established at Tassajara Springs, deep in the wilderness of Monterey County. This mountain retreat was not only the first Buddhist monastery for Westerners, it also broke from tradition in allowing men and women, married and single, to practice together. It is the setting of many of the accounts in this book. In November of 1969 Suzuki Roshi left Sokoji to found the City Center on Page Street in San Francisco as a residential Zen practice center. He died there in 1971.

To Suzuki Roshi, the heart of a Zen temple is the *zendo*, or zazen hall. There he would join his students in zazen (often just called "sitting"), formal meals, and services in which *sutras*, Buddhist scripture, were chanted. There he

would also give lectures, sometimes called *dharma* talks.
Dharma is a Sanskrit word for Buddhist teaching. Usually
one or two forty-minute periods of zazen were held early in
the morning and in the evening. Sometimes there would be
sesshin, when zazen would continue from early morning till
night for up to seven days, broken only by brief walking
periods, services, meals, lectures, and short breaks. During
sesshin Suzuki would conduct formal private interviews
with his students called *dokusan*.

Suzuki's main teaching was silent—the way he picked up
a teacup or met someone walking on a path or in a hallway,
or how he joined with his students in work, meals, and
meditation. But when the occasion arose to speak, he made
an impression. This book is a record of such impressions,
each brief exchange stored away in the mind of an individual who carried it along for thirty years or more. Their
glimpses of Suzuki Roshi show that his way was not system-
atic or formulaic. He emphasized that the ungraspable
spirit of Buddhism is what continues, while the expression
of that spirit always changes. The teachings of Buddha, he

said, were for particular moments, people, and situations and were relative and imperfect.

Shunryu Suzuki touched thousands of people, Buddhist and non-Buddhist, many directly and many more through a now well-known collection of his lectures called *Zen Mind, Beginner's Mind.* Today there are small Buddhist groups all over the West, of his lineage and of other lineages, that exist in no small part because of the efforts of this man.

In 1999 I published a biography of Suzuki titled *Crooked Cucumber: The Life and Zen Teaching of Shunryu Suzuki.* I continue to collect the oral history of those times, to interview and correspond with people about their experiences with Suzuki Roshi and Zen practice, and to reflect on what I learned in the five years I studied with him. *To Shine One Corner of the World* is drawn from these records, from Zen Center archives, and from a few other sources.

The title of this book is a well-known phrase from the Lotus Sutra attributed to Shakyamuni Buddha. Suzuki referred to it on a number of occasions, usually translating it "to light up one corner," but in one lecture he said:

We say, to shine one corner of the world—just one corner.
If you shine one corner, then people around you will feel
better. You will always feel as if you are carrying an
umbrella to protect people from heat or rain.

Suzuki Roshi often played with words, and his use of the word "shine" that day may have been a whimsical substitution. It lends itself to various interpretations—as do many of the encounters in this book.

I hope you enjoy the wisdom of Suzuki Roshi; he had great confidence in yours.

David Chadwick
Sebastopol, California, May 29, 2000

moments with Shunryu Suzuki

One morning when we were all sitting zazen, Suzuki Roshi gave a brief impromptu talk in which he said, "Each of you is perfect the way you are . . . and you can use a little improvement."

Once I asked Suzuki Roshi, "What is nirvana?"

He replied: "Seeing one thing through to the end."

One day at Tassajara Suzuki Roshi and a group of students took some tools and walked up a hot, dusty trail to work on a project. When they got to the top, they discovered that they had forgotten a shovel, and the students began a discussion about who should return to get it. After the discussion had ended, they realized that Roshi wasn't there. He was already halfway down the mountain trail, on his way to pick up the shovel.

One day I complained to Suzuki Roshi about the people I was working with.

He listened intently. Finally, he said, "If you want to see virtue, you have to have a calm mind."

A student asked in dokusan, "If a tree falls in the forest and no one hears it, does it make a sound?"

Suzuki Roshi answered, "It doesn't matter."

It was my first sesshin and, before the first day was over, I was convinced I couldn't make it. My husband's turn for dokusan came that afternoon. He asked Suzuki Roshi to see me instead.

"This is all a mistake," I told Roshi. "I can't do this; I just came to be with my husband."

"There is no mistake," he insisted. "You may leave, of course, but there's no place to go."

One day a student was in the hall at Sokoji when Suzuki Roshi approached him.

"Just to be alive is enough," Suzuki said, and with that, he turned around and walked away.

One night after a dharma talk, I asked Suzuki Roshi a question about life and death. The answer he gave made my fear of death, for that moment, pop like a bubble.

He looked at me and said, "You will always exist in the universe in some form."

Once in a lecture, Suzuki Roshi said, "We should practice zazen like someone who is dying. For him, there is nothing to rely on. When you reach this kind of understanding, you will not be fooled by anything."

A student at Tassajara sat facing Suzuki Roshi on a tatami mat in his room. The student said he couldn't stop snacking in the kitchen and asked what he should do.

Suzuki reached under his table. "Here, have some jelly beans," he said.

A student, filled with emotion and crying, implored, "Why is there so much suffering?"

Suzuki Roshi replied, "No reason."

At a question session with Suzuki Roshi at Sokoji, a young man asked, "What should a Zen practitioner do with his spare time?"

Suzuki at first looked perplexed and repeated the phrase, "Spare time?" He repeated it again and then began to laugh uproariously.

A student of Suzuki Roshi's, a publisher of Beat poetry, saw his teacher of a year and a half in a private interview. He said that he couldn't continue, that every time he sat zazen he started to cry. "I can't take it," he said. "I'm leaving. I can't be here anymore."

Suzuki didn't tell him to stay. He merely said, "You try and you try and you fail, and then you go deeper."

I was driving Suzuki Roshi and a fellow student back to Sokoji from the Mill Valley Zendo. My friend, who was in the back seat, his Camel cigarettes in his shirt pocket, asked Suzuki a question about Zen.

"Zen is hard," Suzuki said. "It's at least as hard as quitting smoking."

A well-known Japanese Rinzai Zen master dropped by Sokoji to meet Suzuki Roshi. After they chanted a sutra together, the visiting priest asked to see a sutra book on the altar. He looked at it, then suddenly exploded, stamping his foot on the floor and shouting, "This is not Zen!" He tore the book in two and threw it on the floor.

Suzuki squatted down and picked up the pieces. "Oh, this sutra book was donated to the temple when there was a memorial service for an old woman from a different sect," he said. "We accept everything here. We chant everything. We eat everything." For a moment the guest still looked angry. Then Suzuki said, "Let's go have some tea." A friendship began that continued as long as they were both alive.

Once a student asked Suzuki Roshi, "Why do you have forty-minute zazen periods, when most Zen teachers in America have only thirty? My legs really hurt when I sit for forty minutes. Won't you consider having thirty-minute periods, at least in sesshin?"

Suzuki replied, "That's very interesting. I've been thinking that we should have fifty-minute periods." After a pregnant pause, he added, "But maybe we can compromise. Let's make it forty minutes."

I was struggling with questions about the meaning, if any, of life and death, and I told Suzuki Roshi that I was engaged in an existential philosophical quest. I told him how absorbing and exciting it was for me and asked him if I was on the right track.

He said, "There is no end to that kind of search."

One day in a lecture Suzuki Roshi said, "When you see one leaf falling, you may say, Oh, autumn is here! One leaf is not just one leaf; it means the whole autumn. Here you already understand the all-pervading power of your practice. Your practice covers everything."

A student asked, "Is enlightenment a complete remedy?"

Suzuki Roshi replied, "No."

During a break in one of the early sesshins at
Sokoji, a student returning to his seat early
straightened a picture on the wall before he sat down
on his cushion. Only he and Suzuki Roshi were in
the zendo at the time. After a moment, Suzuki got up
to leave the room. He walked down the aisle, stopped
at the picture, returned it to its crooked position, and
continued out the door.

While serving as Suzuki Roshi's attendant, I arrived at his cabin at Tassajara and found him in his underwear scrubbing out the toilet. "I should be doing that," I said, with some embarrassment.

"Sit down and have some tea," he answered.

A flamboyant young man with long hair and beads around his neck had been trying hard to practice Zen at Sokoji while continuing his hippie lifestyle. One day he asked Suzuki Roshi a question about marijuana and Zen, to which Suzuki answered, "Maybe you smoke too much marijuana."

"Okay," the fellow said, "I'll quit. You're the boss."

"No!" Suzuki said. "*You're* the boss!"

A student asked, "Does a Zen master suffer in a different way than his students suffer?"

Suzuki Roshi answered, "In the same way. If not, I don't think he is good enough."

One day while editing a transcription of Suzuki Roshi's first lecture on the *Sandokai*, I came upon the phrase "things as it is." I asked him if perhaps he had not meant to say "things as they are," which I thought to be proper syntax.

"No," he said, "what I meant is 'things as it is.'"

One morning at the Haiku Zendo in Los Altos, a group was sitting around the breakfast table drinking coffee, and a student asked Suzuki Roshi, "What is hell?"

"Hell is having to read aloud in English," he answered.

During his first dokusan, a student said he couldn't stop thinking during meditation.

Suzuki Roshi asked, "Is there some problem with thinking?"

Suzuki Roshi's answer to my "What is enlightenment?" question was to laugh and say, "You see?
It's the monkey mind! Trying to understand
enlightenment with the monkey mind!"

Once in a lecture Suzuki Roshi said, "Hell is not punishment, it's training."

On the fourth day of sesshin, as we sat with our painful legs, aching backs, hopes, and doubts about whether it was worth it, Suzuki Roshi began his talk by saying slowly, "The problems you are now experiencing . . ."

"Will go away," we were sure he was going to say.

". . . will continue for the rest of your life," he concluded.

The way he said it, we all laughed.

Suzuki Roshi said during a talk that some of us wanted to be Zen masters, and that this was very foolish. He said that he wished he was like us, just starting out. "Maybe you think you are green apples hanging on a tree, waiting to ripen so that you can be Buddhas," he said, "but I think you are already ripe, perfect Buddhas now, ready to be picked."

One day during a tea break a student standing next to Suzuki Roshi asked, "So what do you think about all of us crazy Zen students?"

Roshi said, "I think you're all enlightened, until you open your mouth."

Next to the temple on Bush Street was a grocery store run by an old woman. Suzuki Roshi used to buy the old vegetables there. Finally one day the woman said, "Here are some fresh ones. Why don't you take them?"

"The fresh ones will be bought anyway," he answered.

One morning in the zendo as we were all silently sitting zazen, Suzuki Roshi said, "Don't move. Just die over and over. Don't anticipate. Nothing can save you now, because this is your last moment. Not even enlightenment will help you now, because you have no other moments. With no future, be true to yourself—and don't move."

"When you prescribed a year at this place for me, you told me I would find great joy," a student said to Suzuki Roshi, as they sat sipping tea in Suzuki's cabin at Tassajara. "To find that great joy, I will first have to lose the will to live, won't I, Roshi?"

"Yes," he said, "but without gaining a will to die."

My family and I returned to San Francisco after being away from the Zen Center for a year. When I saw Suzuki Roshi I said, "I think I got a little lost."

He replied, "You can never get lost."

During one sesshin at Tassajara it was very cold in the unheated zendo. After a lecture, a student said, "Roshi, I thought you said that when it got cold we'd figure out how to stay warm within our zazen."

Suzuki Roshi answered, "It's just not cold enough yet."

"Suzuki Roshi, I've been listening to your lectures for years," a student said during the question-and-answer time following a lecture, "but I just don't understand. Could you just please put it in a nutshell? Can you reduce Buddhism to one phrase?"

Everyone laughed. Suzuki laughed.

"Everything changes," he said. Then he asked for another question.

During a break on the fourth day of a sesshin at Tassajara, I stood on the bridge overlooking the creek. It was a beautiful fall day. The leaves on the trees were all vibrating and alive, and I could see energy coursing through everything.

Suzuki Roshi came by, looked in my eyes, and said, "Stay exactly like that."

A student told Suzuki Roshi about an experience in which he had dissolved into amazing spaciousness.

"Yes, you could call that enlightenment," Suzuki said, "but it's best to forget about it. And how's your work coming?"

My friend and I were summer guests at Tassajara. I was initiating him into the rigors of the hot baths, putting on the act of a drill instructor. The only other person in the water was a small man whose feet almost didn't touch bottom. He joined in our routine until we were all laughing. Later we entered the stream, which was full of hungry, inch-long fish. Every few seconds one of them would take a nibble.

Later that evening there was a lecture by the abbot, Suzuki Roshi, whom I recognized as the little man from the baths. In his talk he said that Zen students should be like feeding fish in their practice, nothing more, and he made his mouth and hand move like the mouths of the small fish.

Now and then Suzuki Roshi would make this point: "In the Lotus Sutra, Buddha says to light up one corner—not the whole world. Just make it clear where you are."

Suzuki Roshi washed his feet on the doorstep after working in the garden. His attendant, who was standing just inside the door, handed him a towel. She then reached down and pinched one of his toes.

"That is one of the powers of Buddha," he said.

"What is?"

"To see what someone needs and give it to them."

In dokusan a student repeated something that Suzuki Roshi had said in a lecture.

Suzuki shook his head.

"No?" the student asked, "but you said . . . "

"When I said it, it was true," Suzuki answered. "When you said it, it was false."

A student remembers a lecture where Suzuki Roshi said, "If it's not paradoxical, it's not true."

On a visit to the East Coast, Suzuki Roshi arrived at the meeting place of the Cambridge Buddhist Society to find everyone scrubbing down the interior in anticipation of his visit. They were surprised to see him, because he had written that he would arrive on the following day.

He tied back the sleeves of his robe and insisted on joining the preparations "for the grand day of my arrival."

After an evening lecture a man in the audience asked, "You say that Zen is everywhere. So why do we have to come to the Zen Center?"

"Zen is everywhere," Suzuki Roshi agreed. "But for you, Zen is right here."

One day a student asked, "Roshi, I have a lot of sexual desire. I'm thinking of becoming celibate. Should I try to limit myself in this way?"

"Sex is like brushing your teeth," Suzuki answered. "It's a good thing to do, but not so good to do it all day long."

Suzuki Roshi had asked his students at Tassajara to practice counting their breaths, a traditional method of meditating, over the ninety-day training period. Many people found it difficult. Their questions to him revealed that they saw it as a technique, one they hoped they would perfect someday.

In lecture Suzuki said, "When you count your breathing: one, two, three . . . it means 'right now, right now, right now.' It means that you never lose your practice. You will not be so rigid as to try to do it in the future, but right now."

A student asked Suzuki Roshi if he kept an eye on his students to see if they were following the precepts, the Buddhist guidelines of conduct.

"I don't pay any attention to whether you're following the precepts or not," he answered. "I just notice how you are with one another."

One day in lecture Suzuki Roshi said, "When you are completely absorbed in your breathing, there is no self. What is your breathing? That breathing is not you, nor air. What is it? It is not self at all. When there is no self, you have absolute freedom. Because you have a silly idea of self, you have a lot of problems."

While helping Suzuki Roshi to prepare for a marriage ceremony, I said, "Roshi, I don't understand. You recite the same thing at every wedding. You say to the man, 'You have married the perfect wife,' and then you say to the wife, 'You have married the perfect husband.' You say that no matter who it is."

He smiled at me mischievously and said, "Oh, you don't understand?"

A brief verse that has always been recited at the Zen Center goes like this:

Great robe of liberation / Field far beyond form and emptiness /Wearing Buddha's teaching / Saving all beings.

In the early sixties this was chanted only in Japanese. No one knew what it meant. One day a student went to Suzuki Roshi and asked, "What's the meaning of that chant we do right after zazen?" Suzuki said, "I don't know." Katagiri Sensei, his assistant teacher, started going through the drawers looking for a translation. Suzuki gestured to him to stop. Then he turned to the student, pointed to his heart, and said, "It's love."

The monks at a Japanese training temple had questioned a student of Suzuki Roshi's about the validity of the student's ordination. They said that it wasn't real, because he hadn't gone through the proper ceremony, hadn't done any monk's begging, and hadn't had his head shaved or received robes until he arrived in Japan.

"So, am I a monk or not a monk?" he asked Suzuki.

"Things go the way the mind goes," Suzuki told him. "If you think you're a monk, you're a monk. If you don't think so, you're not a monk."

Suzuki Roshi usually encouraged me, because I was so down on myself, but once after a one-day sitting, for the first time, I was feeling proud of myself. I went to him and said, "Now I can count every breath. What do I do next?"

He leaned forward and said to me fiercely, "Don't ever think that you can sit zazen! That's a big mistake! Zazen sits zazen!"

In the middle of a sesshin Suzuki Roshi spoke in a lecture about the pain that everyone was experiencing, especially in their legs, from the long hours of sitting. "Pain is your teacher," he said.

Later that day in dokusan a student started talking to him about how much she felt she was growing because of trying to master pain.

He stopped her and said, "Pain is tedious."

Suzuki Roshi often said we shouldn't have "a gaining idea" or any idea of attainment. I once asked him why anybody would do zazen if they didn't have a gaining idea.

He said, "You still have one gaining idea."

"What is that?" I wanted to know.

He replied, "That's a secret."

A woman told Suzuki Roshi she found it difficult to mix Zen practice with the demands of being a housewife. "I feel I am trying to climb a ladder. But for every step upward, I slip backward two steps."

"Forget the ladder," Suzuki told her. "In Zen everything is right here on the ground."

Once while driving Suzuki Roshi back to San Francisco from Los Altos, I asked him if there was much hope for that handful of middle-aged, suburban housewives to accomplish anything as Zen students. After all, I thought, they only sat together once a week, unlike we students, who sat daily at Zen Center.

He told me their understanding was "actually pretty good," and he noted, "They don't seem to suffer from arrogance."

At a Sokoji lecture a distraught woman said she had been rejected by a Zen teacher in Los Angeles. Suzuki Roshi told her that if she went back to that teacher he would accept her.

"Now *you* reject me," she cried.

"Oh no," Suzuki said, with sincere sympathy in his voice, "you can stay here." And with his arms opened and long robe sleeves gracefully hanging at his sides, he took a step toward her and added, "I never reject anybody."

I had dokusan with Suzuki Roshi during sesshin. I felt lost and far from home at that point in my life, and I asked him if big mind was lost in the dark, too.

He said, "No, not lost in the dark, working in the dark!" and he moved his arms about, demonstrating. He said it was like the many-armed statue of Avaloki-teshvara, and he made the statue come to life for a moment.

When I first came to the temple I asked to learn zazen, but Suzuki Roshi didn't have time that day. I frequently returned, but for two months Suzuki refused to teach me. Then one day he took me to a remote part of the building and said, "Now would you like to learn zazen?" After teaching me attention to posture and breathing, he gave me a book. Many years later I asked him why he had refused to teach me zazen when I first asked for it.

He said, "I did not want to spoil what is naturally present."

There was a big boulder in the Tassajara creek that Suzuki Roshi said he wanted for his rock garden. Every day four or five of us went down to the creek during the silent work period and struggled to move the boulder by various devices and means. Each one of us was secure in the knowledge that somehow we were going to move that stone to his rock garden, which was quite a distance away. After a week the rock hadn't budged, but no one was about to break the silence or give up. One day Suzuki Roshi came down to the creek and struggled along with us. Some visitors called down from the bridge to ask what we were doing.

Suzuki Roshi called up, "We don't know!"

"Roshi, what is the difference between you and me?" I asked, as we drank tea together.

"I have students and you don't," he answered without hesitation.

A student asked Suzuki Roshi why the Japanese make their teacups so thin and delicate that they break easily.

"It's not that they're too delicate," he answered, "but that you don't know how to handle them. You must adjust yourself to the environment, and not vice versa."

As Suzuki Roshi was walking out of the building to meet his ride to Los Altos, a woman at the top of the steps called out to the driver, "You be careful now; we don't want to lose our treasure!"

Suzuki turned, made a loud SMACK! with his hands, and called out, "No more!" He threw his head back and laughed and continued to laugh as the car drove off.

I hope you are enjoying

the wisdom of the Buddha.

During the question-and-answer period after a sesshin lecture, someone said to Suzuki Roshi, "Here I sit near the end of this session, energized and thinking that there is a lot of power in this practice."

Suzuki replied, "Don't use it."

During a formal silent lunch in the zendo, a young woman with a soup tureen stopped in front of Suzuki Roshi, gave him two ladles full, and blurted out, "Suzuki Roshi, when I'm serving you soup, what is it like for you?"

He said, "It's like you're serving your whole being to me in this bowl."

Someone at a lecture asked Suzuki Roshi about psychoanalysis.

In answer he said, "You think the mind is like a pond that you throw things in, and they sink to the bottom, like old shoes, and later they rise to the surface. But actually, there's no such thing as the mind!"

One Saturday morning a student arrived late for the beginning of a sesshin. He was Suzuki Roshi's first ordained student to wear the traditional priest's robe, the *okesa*, in America. After breakfast Suzuki took him to task saying, "Priests don't arrive late! You're no priest! You have no right to wear that okesa!"

The student was mortified and started to take off his robe.

"What are you doing?" said Suzuki. "No one has the right to tell you to take off the okesa."

During a lecture Suzuki Roshi had said that life was impossible.

"If it's impossible, how can we do it?" a student asked.

"You do it every day," Suzuki answered.

Zen Center was a magnet for sixties countercul-
ture arrivals to the San Francisco Bay area. An
older woman asked Suzuki Roshi if he felt any pressure and difficulty with the various ragged, long-
haired students who came off the street seeking
enlightenment.

"I am very grateful for them," he said. "I will do all I
can for them."

A young woman went to Suzuki Roshi and showed him a twenty-dollar bill she'd just found on the sidewalk in Japantown. She told him she couldn't decide what to do with it. "Should I give it to charity, put up a note on a telephone pole and wait, or just keep it?" she asked him.

"Here," he said, "I'll take it," and he put it in the sleeve of his robe.

I asked Suzuki Roshi for advice before leaving for Japan in the summer of 1969. He said, "When you go to my temple, there is nothing to see."

A young woman wearing many strings of beads raised her hand when Suzuki asked for questions. "Suzuki Roshi, what is sex?"

"Once you say sex, everything is sex," he answered.

One evening in a lecture Suzuki Roshi said, "If you're not a Buddhist, you think there are Buddhists and non-Buddhists. But if you're a Buddhist, you realize everybody's a Buddhist—even the bugs."

Asked why there was a rule of silence during most meals, Suzuki Roshi answered, "You cannot eat and talk at the same time."

During a formal question-and-answer ceremony called *shosan*, Suzuki Roshi responded to a student's question, and the student started to get up from kneeling. Then Suzuki added slowly and deliberately, "The most important thing . . . is . . . to . . . find . . . out . . . what . . . is . . . the . . . most important thing."

Soon after she had arrived in America to join her husband, Suzuki Roshi's wife said, "Why do you work so hard preparing for lecture? It's raining, and the last night that it rained only two people came. I hope that ten come tonight."

He answered, "One or ten, it makes no difference!"

Apsychologist asked about the nature of enlightenment.

"I'm not enlightened," Suzuki Roshi said. "I can't answer."

As I was telling Suzuki Roshi what a disaster my life had become, he began to chuckle. I found myself laughing along with him. There was a pause. I asked him what I should do.

"Sit zazen," he replied. "Life without zazen is like winding your clock without setting it. It runs perfectly well, but it doesn't tell time."

The first time I met Suzuki Roshi, I told him I did not feel that I necessarily fit in with Soto Zen, which is all about sitting zazen. I said my way to the top of the mountain was not sitting but the way of the arts, of tea ceremony, and *sumi-e.*

He said, "Sitting has nothing to do with it!"

A student told Suzuki Roshi, "Sometimes I get lethargic and discouraged about life and Zen practice."

"This is good," Suzuki answered. "All practice has these moments."

While driving my teacher to the City Center from Tassajara, I said, "Suzuki Roshi, may I ask you a question?" and he said yes. I proceeded to beg him to tell me what I should do to understand reality, to become enlightened. I told him that I was totally dedicated, and that whatever he told me, I would do. I went on and on, making sure that he was thoroughly aware of my sincerity and devotion.

I turned to him for an answer. He was sound asleep.

During a discussion, someone asked Suzuki Roshi if he ate meat.

"Yes, I do," he replied.

"Buddha didn't eat any meat."

"Yes, Buddha was a very pious man."

"Whether you sit zazen or not, something wonderful will happen to you," Suzuki Roshi said to me in dokusan. "Actually, this will happen someday to everyone. If you keep up your zazen and practice, when you have this wonderful experience it will continue forever. But if you don't cultivate yourself in this way, it will pass, like a psychedelic experience."

In the old days, during sesshin, Suzuki Roshi would encourage us to not change positions while sitting. He would say, "Don't move. Don't chicken out." But he also said, "When I say don't move, it doesn't mean you can't move."

Once when talking about going to the beach and looking out at the ocean, Suzuki Roshi reflected, "If you're alert, you can hear the tide turn."

A student confided in Suzuki Roshi that she had tremendous feelings of love for him, and that it confused her.

"Don't worry," he said. "You can let yourself have all the feelings you have for your teacher. That's good. I have enough discipline for both of us."

One evening at Tassajara I was with Suzuki Roshi outside his cabin. In the slanting moonlight his garden and its individual rocks seemed more beautiful than ever to me, magical. "What a beautiful garden you've made!" I said.

"Oh. If you like it so much, why don't you take it with you? You can have it," he said.

"I don't think I could move it," I answered, "and I'd never get it all back together again quite this way."

"Sure, you take it," he said. "Put it up on the roof of that cabin over there."

One time I was at Sokoji in the afternoon on some business, when Suzuki Roshi asked to see the cherry blossoms that were in bloom at the Japanese Tea Garden in Golden Gate Park. I had never been alone with him before outside the temple. All the way there he said nothing but just sat calmly looking out at the passing scene. As I drove up to the garden, and the profusion of pink blossoms came into view, he simply gazed at them for a moment, then said, "Very beautiful. Let's go back now."

I went in for my meeting with Suzuki Roshi during sesshin. At that time my main purpose was to get him to approve of me. I told him how I was trying hard to do the right thing. He listened carefully, without judgment.

"You get a gold star," he said.

Suzuki Roshi said that, if he scolded you in front of others, not to feel too bad, because it might be intended for someone else who wasn't ready to hear it. "If I hit you with the stick, it's because I trust you, because you're a good student. Sometimes it's for you, sometimes it's for the person next to you."

At Suzuki Roshi's prompting I kept a journal about my Zen practice, and every week we'd go over it. Once I wrote about being his driver. Should I keep driving him to Los Altos on Thursdays, or should I bring up at a meeting that others could share this privilege. I concluded my entry with, "I'm making such a problem out of this, aren't I?"

He wrote below that: "Speak no word. Do no doing."

A group of us had lunch with Suzuki Roshi in New York City. People were wondering how we should treat this religious man, and how we should act. Very early on in the lunch, he put a napkin on his head and sat there with it. Then we all put our napkins on our heads. He made everybody feel comfortable.

After a lecture in a home, when the group was having tea, the host handed Suzuki Roshi a card and said, "Here is my understanding of your lecture." On the card was written "$0 = 1 = \infty$."

"That's good," Roshi told him. "The last figure is usually overlooked."

During a lecture in which Suzuki Roshi was talking about the precepts, he said: "Do not steal. When we think we do not possess something, then we want to steal. But actually everything in the world belongs to us, so there is no need to steal. For example, my glasses. They are just glasses. They do not belong to me or to you, or they belong to all of us. But you know about my tired old eyes, and so you let me use them."

A student got discouraged because the higher states he experienced always passed. "What's the use?" he asked.

Suzuki Roshi laughed and said, "That's right, no use. All these states come and go, but if you continue your practice, you find there's something underneath."

A student at Tassajara told Suzuki Roshi that the monastic schedule was hard on her. She said that she always felt sleepy in zazen and asked if it wouldn't be a good idea to add more time for sleep to the schedule, so that people could be more alert in meditation.

Suzuki answered, "When you're tired, your ego is tired."

In the early days there were no snacks in the kitchen at Tassajara, so sometimes I'd send cookies to a friend of mine there. I began to wonder why she didn't write to say how great I was. Then I thought, how selfish of me. I'm not being generous; there are strings attached. I just want something back.

I told Suzuki Roshi about this, and he said, "It's all right for you to take care of her, but first you have to take care of yourself!" His voice rose as he said this, and then he got right in my face to say loudly, "Do you understand?"

One morning in zazen, Suzuki Roshi broke the silence by saying, "You're like loaves of bread, loaves of bread baking in the oven."

We were all fascinated with the notion of enlightenment, but Suzuki Roshi said it was not the point that needed emphasis. Once, in an interview, I decided to address the matter directly. "I am here to be enlightened," I said.

He shot me a piercing glance and then quietly replied, "If your practice continues, enlightenment will come. But even if it does not, if your practice is good, it is almost the same."

A student said, "I compare myself to other students and feel inadequate. I haven't read anything about Buddhism."

"Oh! That's the best way to come to practice," Suzuki Roshi answered.

One day I complained to Suzuki Roshi that my mind would not be still. It chattered at me constantly during zazen.

"When your back gets straight, your mind will become quiet," he answered.

"Why do you shave your head?" a visitor asked Suzuki Roshi after a lecture at Sokoji.

Suzuki rubbed his head and answered, "It's the fundamental hair style!"

A clinical psychiatrist questioned Suzuki Roshi about consciousness.

"I don't know anything about consciousness," Suzuki said. "I just try to teach my students how to hear the birds sing."

After a lecture a young man asked Suzuki Roshi what he thought about LSD.

All he said was, "Enlightenment is not a state of mind."

Often when he was speaking, Suzuki Roshi would look around and ask, "Do you understand?"

Once I remember that he added, "If you think you do, you don't!"

One day during a lecture, a stranger sat in zazen posture in the front, very close to Suzuki Roshi. He mimicked Roshi's movements, made weird facial expressions and threatening gestures. He blew toward the candle burning behind Suzuki Roshi. Roshi took no notice of him. When Roshi got up to leave, he did his usual bows, turned, then whirled back and quickly blew out the candle. He walked up the aisle, laughing to himself.

One night I was on desk duty in the front hall of the City Center. Suzuki Roshi and his wife were going out. I was a new student, sitting stiffly. He smiled and said, "Good night."

That's all that happened, but it changed my life.

Speaking on the precept barring the use of intoxi-
cants, Suzuki Roshi gave it a surprising interpre-
tation. "This means don't sell Buddhism. Not only
liquor but also spiritual teaching is intoxicating."

Suzuki Roshi was at Tassajara when his youngest son, Otohiro, who had never done Zen practice, had just finished a grueling three-day initiatory sitting. Otohiro came to Roshi's cabin and there was a brief exchange between father and son in Japanese.

Roshi told me later that Otohiro had said the sitting was a wonderful experience. Although he wanted to congratulate his son, he had felt obliged not to respond with enthusiasm. In that way, Roshi said, his son could properly understand his realization as his own discovery and not as something his father had given him.

One day Suzuki Roshi went with a group of us in a truck to a ranch some miles from Tassajara to pick fruit. We were all trying to be good Zen students—work hard, pick the fruit, pack the boxes. We didn't realize how serious we'd become, until Suzuki Roshi climbed a tree and started throwing fruit at us.

I was laboring to finish my Ph.D. thesis. My job was to go straight to my desk first thing every morning. Once in a while, from peer pressure or an unwillingness to face my typewriter, I would wander over to Zen Center and sit in the zendo.

Invariably, Suzuki Roshi would come up and tap me on the shoulder, wrinkle his forehead, point toward my apartment, and whisper, "Why aren't you over there writing the thesis?"

During the Saturday morning work period at Sokoji, a student who'd been around for a few years was sweeping the zendo floor when he saw a newcomer apprehensively wondering what to do. He went over and handed the fellow his broom. When he turned around, there was Suzuki Roshi, arm outstretched, offering him his own broom.

Suzuki Roshi said to me in dokusan, "You're like a rock, a big rock on the path. People don't know what you do, but if they're tired they'll sit on you, and that provides a nice rest for them. Don't paint the rock."

Suzuki Roshi had been quite ill. He had been falsely diagnosed with infectious hepatitis and had gone to the hospital for more tests. I went to visit him just as his lunch was served.

He motioned me to come and sit next to him at the edge of the bed. As I crossed the room, he mouthed the words "I have cancer." When I sat next to him he leaned over and took a bit of food on his fork and put it into my mouth. "Now we can eat off the same plate again." He said it as if the new diagnosis was a gift.

A student who had just concluded a thirty-day zazen retreat with two enthusiastic dharma pals asked Suzuki Roshi how to maintain the extraordinary state of mind he'd attained.

"Concentrate on your breathing, and it will go away," Suzuki said.

A student asked Suzuki Roshi what he thought American Zen would be like in the future.

"Very colorful," he answered.

A young woman asked Suzuki Roshi after a Sokoji talk, "Roshi, sometimes when I'm trying to decide what I should do, I ask myself, 'In this case, what would Roshi do?' Should I continue that practice?"

Suzuki answered, "Then should I also ask myself, 'What would Roshi do?'"

I went up to Suzuki Roshi's room not long before his death. He was in bed, extremely weak, his skin discolored. He bowed, and I did the same. Then he looked right at me and said, not with a loud voice but firmly, "Don't grieve for me. Don't worry. I know who I am."

An evening meeting of all students at Tassajara had gone on for a couple of hours. We had discussed the schedule, the rules, and the importance of maintaining our practice during the upcoming busy guest season. Every so often someone quoted Suzuki Roshi or referred to "Suzuki Roshi's way." The director turned to Suzuki, who had been sitting quietly throughout, and asked if he had something to say.

"Maybe this is already too much talk," he said, and the meeting was over.

My wife and I were agonizing about whether to continue to practice at Tassajara or to leave and raise a family. We decided to talk to Suzuki Roshi about it. He listened to us for a while and then abruptly picked up a brush and ink and wrote five words rapidly on a sheet of paper. I was shocked by his vehemence, and when he handed me the paper, the message struck me like a blow from his stick. Without further discussion we decided to remain at Tassajara.

DO NOT SAY
TOO LATE
May 14 1969
Ren Suzuki

Explanation of Buddhist Terms

Definitions of Buddhist terms in Sanskrit (Skt), Japanese, and English.

Avalokiteshvara (Skt) The mythic/cosmic bodhisattva (enlightenment being) of compassion who hears the cries of the world.

big mind A term Suzuki used for buddha mind, or the mind that
includes everything, as compared to small mind, which is limited
by discrimination and ideas of self.

buddha (Skt) An awakened one, referring both to historic or
mythic persons such as Shakyamuni Buddha and to ultimate,
awakened reality.

dharma (Skt) The teaching, the truth or reality that is taught,
and the path to approach that truth.

dokusan A formal private interview with a teacher, a Soto Zen
term.

emptiness A term denoting the interconnected, relative true nature of all, with nothing having an inherent, fixed, separate nature or existence.

monkey mind Small mind, especially when it is jumping from one thing to another, like a monkey from branch to branch.

nirvana (Skt) In early Buddhism, the cessation of all suffering. In Zen, nirvana is understood as ultimately not separate from everyday life and the worldly cycles of suffering.

okesa The outer patchwork robe traditionally worn by a Buddhist monk.

practice The expression of zazen in daily life.

Rinzai Zen One of the two major sects of Zen.

roshi "Venerable old teacher," a respectful title for priest, or Zen master. Shunryu Suzuki was usually called Suzuki Roshi starting in 1966. Before that, he was usually called Suzuki Sensei or Reverend Suzuki.

sensei Title used for teachers, doctors, sometimes priests, and other respected persons.

sesshin A concentrated zazen retreat of one or more days, usually five or seven.

Soto Zen One of the two main sects of Zen, emphasizing "just sitting" or silent illumination meditation and its application to everyday activity; Shunryu Suzuki's sect.

stick Either the teacher's stick *(nyoi)*, a short, curved stick carried by teachers in formal situations, or a flat one with a rounded handle.

sumi-e Japanese painting done with brush and black ink.

sutra (Skt) Discourses of the Buddha, old Buddhist scriptures, or scriptures to be chanted.

tatami Japanese rigid straw floor mats approximately two inches thick, three feet wide, and six feet long.

tea ceremony (chanoyu) A formal, aesthetic method of preparing and serving tea, originating in Japan around the sixteenth century.

zazen Zen meditation, sitting meditation. Usually practiced sitting cross-legged on a cushion but can be done in a chair, while walking, chanting, or in any activity. In sitting zazen the practitioner sits upright and still with the eyes half opened, following the breath, counting from one to ten with the breath, concentrating on the lower abdomen or a mantra or a koan (Zen question), or "just sitting" and letting thoughts come and go without attaching to them.

Zen A school of Buddhism originating in China that emphasizes zazen, direct insight, and actual experience of Buddhist truth in everyday activity.

zendo A Zen meditation hall, zazen hall.

Notes

The people listed below are the sources of the accounts in this book. The Introduction has more information on the venues. Rinso-in is Shunryu Suzuki's temple in Yaizu, Japan. More on Shunryu Suzuki, his students, and this book can be found on the web site devoted to this work: <www.cuke.com>.

The graphic insert following page 67, "I hope you are enjoying the wisdom of the Buddha," was written circa 1970 by Shunryu Suzuki with a brush, on rice paper used to wrap a present he gave to his much loved and mentally disturbed student E. L. Hazelwood. Richard Baker retrieved the crinkled remains from a wastebasket and now has it mounted on a wall at Crestone Zen Mountain Center in southwest Colorado.

To Shine One Corner of the World: David Chadwick, City Center,

1971. Pages: 3. David Chadwick, Tassajara, circa 1968. 4. Mel Weitsman, Sokoji, circa 1965. 5. Rick Fields (RIP), Tassajara, circa 1969. 6. Ed Brown, Tassajara, 1967. 7. Pauline Petchey, Sokoji, 1962. 8. Fran Tribe (RIP), Tassajara, 1967. 9. Mel Weitsman, Sokoji, 1968. 10. Frank Anderton, Tassajara, 1967. 11. David Chadwick, Sokoji, 1969. 12. David Chadwick, Tassajara, 1967. 13. Anonymous, Tassajara, 1971. 14. Edward Van Tassel, Sokoji. 15. Dave Haselwood, Sokoji, 1964. 16. Bob Halpern/David Chadwick, Mill Valley, 1968. 17. Kazemitsu Kato, Sokoji, 1959. 18. Durand Kiefer, Los Altos, circa 1966. 19. Frank Anderton, at Charlotte Selver workshop, San Francisco, 1966. 20. David Chadwick, Tassajara, 1967. 21. David Chadwick, Sokoji, 1969. 22. Richard Baker, Sokoji, 1963. 23. Alan Marlowe (RIP), Tassajara, 1970. 24. Ken Spiker, Sokoji, 1965. 25. Reb Anderson, Sokoji, 1969. 26. Alan Marlowe (RIP), Tassajara, 1970. 27. Barbara Hiestand (RIP), Los Altos, circa 1966. 28. Ed Brown, Sokoji, 1966. 29. Steve Stroud, Tassajara, circa 1969. 30. David Chadwick, Sokoji, 1967. 31. Ed Brown, Tassajara, circa 1969. 32. Frank Anderton, City Center, 1970. 33. David Chadwick, Tassajara, circa 1970. 34. Mitsu Suzuki, San Francisco, circa 1964. 35. Ed Brown, Tassajara, 1969. 36. Durand Kiefer, Tassajara, 1967. 37. Toni (Johansen) McCarty, City Center, 1969. 38. Larry Hansen, Tassajara, circa 1968. 39. Bill Shurtleff, Tassajara, circa 1968.

40. Jerry Fuller (RIP), Tassajara, circa 1968. 41. Ken Sawyer, City Center, 1970. 42. Kent B. Davis, Tassajara, 1969. 43. Bill Kwong, Sokoji, 1965. 44. Louise Pryor, Tassajara, 1967. 45. David Chadwick, Tassajara, 1968. 46. Bill Lane, Tassajara, circa 1968. 47. Elsie Mitchell, Cambridge, Mass., 1963. 48. Ken Spiker, Sokoji, circa 1965. 49. David Chadwick, Sokoji, 1966. 50. David Chadwick, Sokoji, 1969. 51. Diana Hart (Cheryl Hughes), Tassajara, 1970. 52. David Chadwick, Sokoji, 1966. 53. Janet Sturgeon, Tassajara, 1971. 54. Mel Weitsman, Sokoji, 1964. 55. Philip Wilson, Rinso-in, 1966. 56. Blanche Hartman, City Center, 1970. 57. Jane Schneider, Tassajara, 1967. 58. Ken Spiker, Sokoji, circa 1965. 59. Barbara Hiestand (RIP), Los Altos, circa 1966. 60. Bob Halpern, on the way from Sokoji to Los Altos, circa 1967. 61. David Chadwick, Sokoji, 1967. 62. Frank Anderton, City Center, 1969. 63. Rowena Pattee, Sokoji, 1964. 64. Larry Hansen, Tassajara, 1967. 65. Alan Marlowe (RIP), Tassajara, 1970. 66. Pauline Petchey, Rinso-in, 1966. 67. Mark Abrams, City Center, 1970. 70. Jack Van Allen, Sokoji, 1968. 71. Larry Hansen, Tassajara, circa 1967. 72. Ken Spiker, Sokoji, circa 1965. 73. Grahame Petchey, Sokoji, 1964. 74. Stan White, Sokoji, circa 1965. 75. Rowena Pattee, Sokoji, circa 1966. 76. Bob Halpern, Sokoji, 1968. 77. Eva Goldscheid, Sokoji, 1969. 78. David Chadwick, Sokoji, circa 1966. 79. Ken Spiker, Sokoji, circa 1965.

80. David Chadwick, Tassajara, circa 1968. 81. Ed Brown, Tassajara, circa 1968. 82. Mitsu Suzuki, Sokoji, 1962. 83. Richard Baker, City Center, circa 1970. 84. Sydney Walter, City Center, 1970. 85. Peg Anderson, Los Altos, circa 1964. 86. Rick Levine, Tassajara, 1970. 87. David Chadwick, on the road from Tassajara to Sokoji, circa 1968. 88. Stan White, Sokoji, circa 1965. 89. David Chadwick, Tassajara, circa 1969. 90. Mel Weitsman, Tassajara, 1970. 91. Elizabeth Tuomi, Berkeley, circa 1970. 92. Toni (Johansen) McCarty, on the road from Sokoji to Los Altos, circa 1965. 93. Tim Buckley, Tassajara, circa 1968. 94. Mike Dixon, San Francisco, circa 1966. 95. Sue Roberts, Tassajara, 1968. 96. Mel Weitsman, Sokoji, circa 1966. 97. Toni (Johansen) McCarty, Sokoji, circa 1966. 98. Joanne Kyger, New York City, 1967. 99. Durand Kiefer, Shanti, an unaffiliated zendo in Los Gatos, circa 1966. 100. Richard Baker, Tassajara, 1966. 101. Arthur Deikman, City Center, circa 1970. 102. David Chadwick, Tassajara, circa 1969. 103. Blanche Hartman, City Center, 1969. 104. Mel Weitsman, Sokoji, 1966. 105. Lew Richmond, Sokoji, 1968. 106. Louise Pryor, Tassajara, 1967. 107. Alan Marlowe (RIP), Tassajara, 1970. 108. Mel Weitsman, Sokoji, circa 1966. 109. Arthur Deikman, Sokoji, circa 1968. 110. Ken Spiker, Sokoji, circa 1965. 111. Durand Kiefer, Tassajara, 1967. 112. Lew Richmond, Sokoji, 1968. 113. Arnie Kotler, City Center, 1971.

114. David Chadwick, Tassajara, 1966. 115. Bob Halpern, Tassajara, 1967. 116. Sue Roberts, Church Creek Ranch, 1968. 117. J. J. Wilson, Sokoji, circa 1968. 118. Mike Dixon, Sokoji, circa 1966. 119. Stan White, Tassajara, circa 1968. 120. Yvonne Rand, Mt. Zion Hospital, San Francisco, 1971. 121. Arthur Deikman, Tassajara, circa 1970. 122. Richard Baker, Sokoji, circa 1966. 123. Bob Halpern, Sokoji, circa 1968. 124. Stan White, City Center, 1971. 125. David Chadwick, Tassajara, circa 1968. 126. Dan Welch, Tassajara, 1969. 127. The calligraphy by Shunryu Suzuki reproduced on this page and referred to on page 126 now hangs in the meditation room of the home temple of Yvonne Rand in Muir Beach, California.

Further Reading

Baker, Richard. *Original Mind: The Practice of Zen in the West.* Riverhead Books, forthcoming.

Brown, Edward Espe. *Tomato Blessings and Radish Teachings: Recipes and Reflections.* Riverhead Books, 1997.

Chadwick, David. *Crooked Cucumber: The Life and Zen Teaching of Shunryu Suzuki.* Broadway Books, 1999.

———. *Thank You and OK! An American Zen Failure in Japan.* Penguin Arkana, 1994.

Fields, Rick. *How the Swans Came to the Lake: A Narrative History of Buddhism in America.* Shambhala, 1992.

Hiestand, Barbara, editor. *Chronicles of Haiku Zendo.* Haiku Zendo Foundation, 1973.

Kaye, Les. *Zen at Work: A Zen Teacher's 30-Year Journey in Corporate America.* Crown, 1996.

Mitchell, Elsie. *Sun Buddhas, Moon Buddhas: A Zen Quest.* Weatherhill, 1973.

Mountain, Marian. *The Zen Environment: The Impact of Zen Meditation.* William Morrow, 1982.

Richmond, Lewis. *Work as a Spiritual Practice: A Practical Buddhist Approach to Inner Growth and Satisfaction on the Job.* Broadway Books, 1999.

Schneider, David. *Street Zen: The Life and Work of Issan Dorsey.* Shambhala, 1993.

Storlie, Erik. *Nothing on My Mind: Berkeley, LSD, Two Zen Masters, and Life on the Dharma Trail.* Shambhala, 1997.

Suzuki, Mitsu. *Temple Dusk: Zen Haiku.* Parallax Press, 1992.

Suzuki, Shunryu. *Branching Streams Flow in the Darkness: Lectures on the Sandokai.* University of California Press, 1999.

———. *Zen Mind, Beginner's Mind.* Weatherhill, 1970.

Tipton, Steve. *Getting Saved from the Sixties.* University of California Press, 1982.

Wenger, Michael. *Thirty-three Fingers: A Collection of Modern American Koans.* Clear Glass Publishing, 1994.

Wind Bell (publication of the San Francisco Zen Center), 1961-2000.

Acknowledgments

I would like to thank the following writers who suggested I do this book: the late wonderful Rick Fields, Lew Richmond, Kazuaki Tanahashi, and Michael Toms of New Dimensions Radio.

I would like to thank those whose memories of encounters with Shunryu Suzuki are related herein. Their names can be found in the notes to the book. And thanks to all those who shared their memories that were not used (for an almost complete list of them, see acknowledgments in *Crooked Cucumber: The Life and Zen Teaching of Shunryu Suzuki,* Broadway Books, 1999).

I would like to thank my agent, friend, and mentor Michael Katz for all the time and effort he put into every stage of the realization of this book. He even wrote his own acknowledgment.

At Broadway Books I would like to thank my editor, Ann Campbell, her assistant, Amanda Gross, Tracy Behar for her initial interest and sealing the deal, and Rebecca Holland in Production. Thanks to Holly Hammond for copyediting.

For reading the vignettes over, helping me to choose which

ones to use, for feedback, suggestions, and in some cases with other assistance, I would also like to thank: Richard Baker, Kamala Buckner, Cha Yu, Elin Chadwick, Kelly Chadwick, Diana Hart, Linda Hess, Jane Hirshfield, Joan Hanley, Niels Holm, Bill Lane, Balthasar Lohmeyer, Heather McFarlin, Elsie Mitchell, Stephen Mitchell, Thomas Moore, Grahame Petchey, Valerie Robin, Renée Roehl, Ken Sawyer, Elizabeth Sawyer, Sahn Bul, Judy Sandors, Peter Schneider, John Sumser, Steve Tipton, Elizabeth Tuomi, Sojun Mel Weitsman, Dan Welch, Michael Wenger, Clare Whitfield, Carol Williams, and Yasodhara.

Thanks to Jenny Wunderly for the design and production. For other help in that area, thanks to David Bullen, Michael Katz, and Raymond Rimmer.

Thanks to Kobun and Katrin Otogawa for the calligraphy on the title page, the character *hikari,* which means light, or to shine.

For other assistance: Catherine Anderson, John Bermel, Tim Buckley, Ahdel Chadwick, Clayton Chadwick, Gil Fronsdal, Daya Goldschlag, Francine de Gruchy, Taigen Dan Leighton, Tano Maida, Maggie McGill, Hideko Petchey, Pauline Petchey, Yvonne Rand, Bill Redican, Diana Rowan, Bill Schwob, Mickey Stunkard, William Shinker, and Dan Welch.

So many people gave me assistance of one kind or another in the development of this book. My apologies to those whom I have forgotten to mention.